Rainer Strzolka

The secret garden
With the Petzval Lens on the go

Hannover Berlin Soderstorf
Galerie für Kulturkommunikation
2024

Petzval lenses are among the optical revolutions in photography, as they were the first to be precisely calculated and fast. One disadvantage was that the images were only sharp in the center and became increasingly blurred towards the edges.

In the meantime, these lenses have been rediscovered for artistic photography. There are some very expensive replicas of the originals. However, it is easy to convert lenses of the Zeiss Biotar type.

This exhibition catalog shows some examples of such photographs with conversions. The exhibition took place in May 2024 on a farm in Lower Saxony, Germany.
All the examples shown here were given away to visitors at the end of the exhibition.
Filmmaterial was Ferrania P30.
Lab: Rainer Strzolka and Foto Weckbrodt Hannover

Please also visit us on the Internet at
www.galerie-fuer-kulturkommunikation.de

The English-language edition is not completely identical to the German-language edition

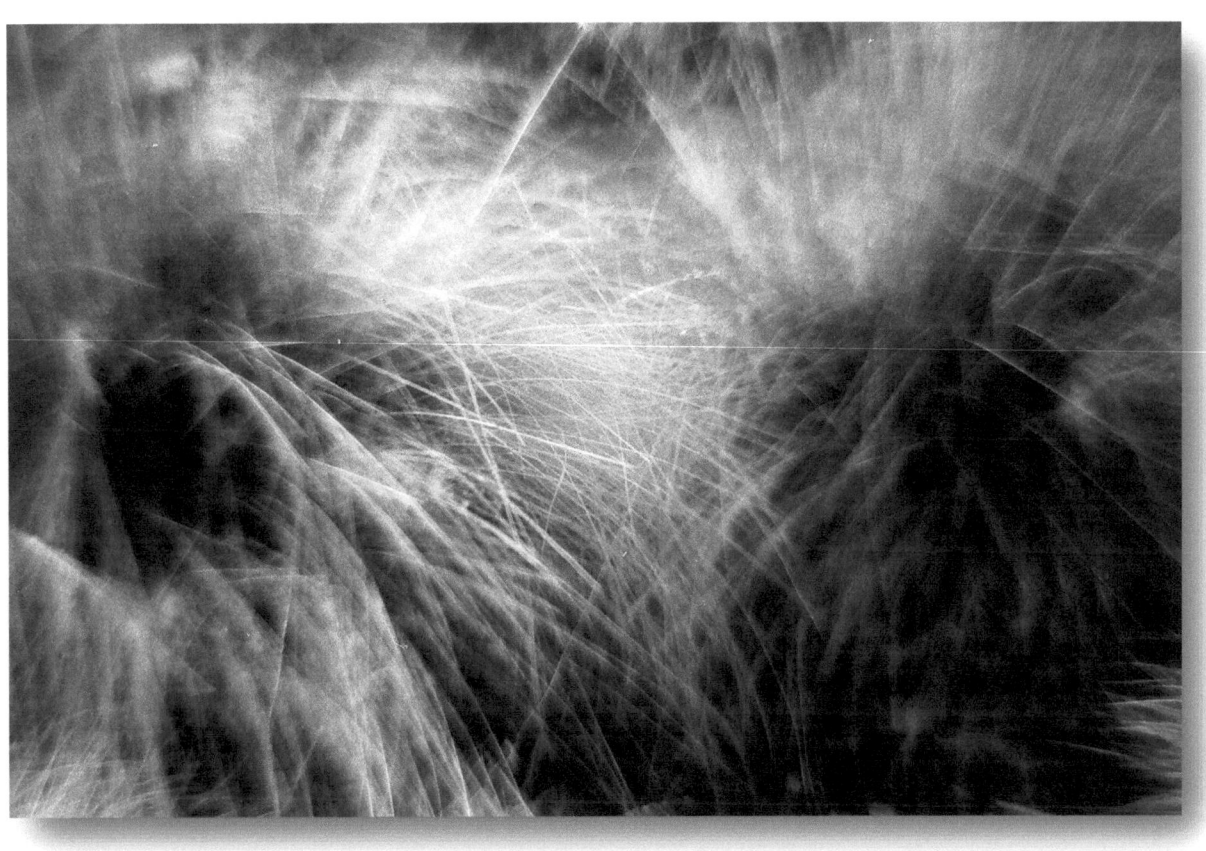

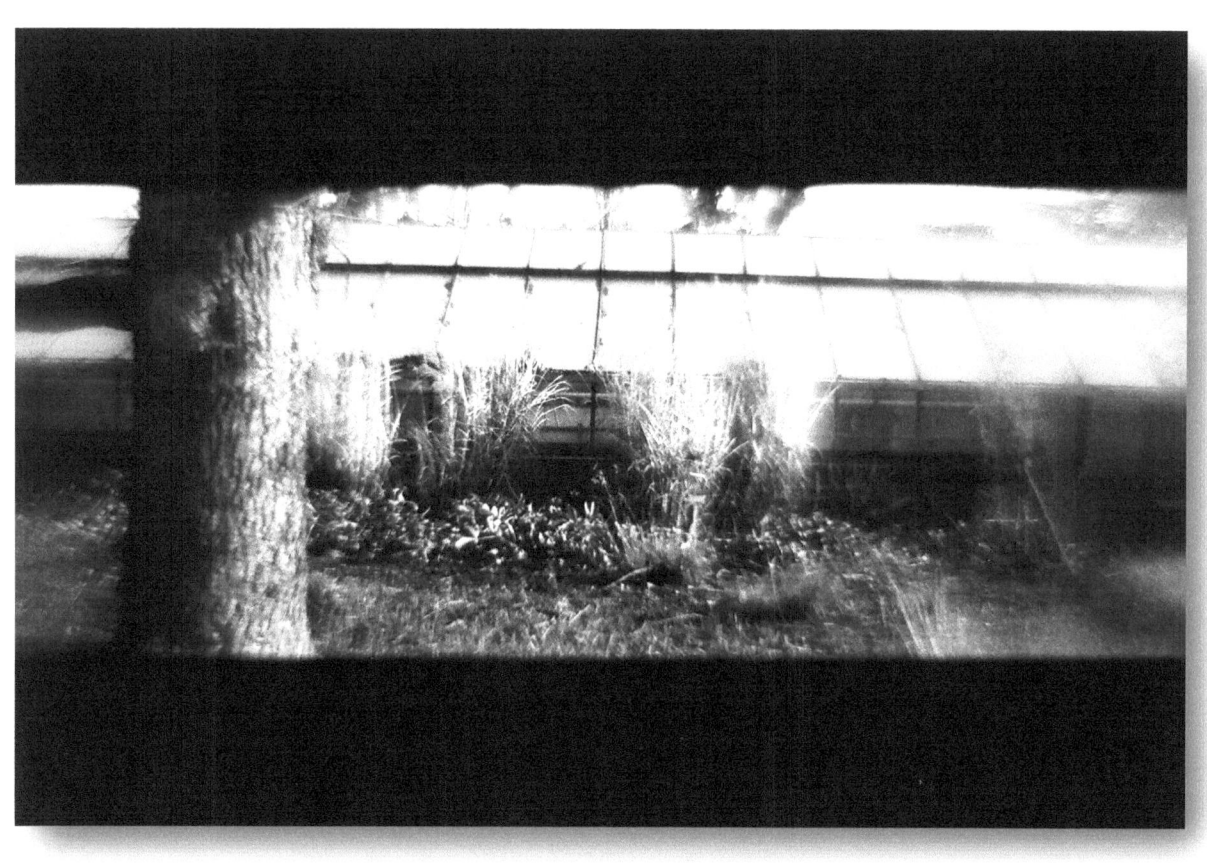

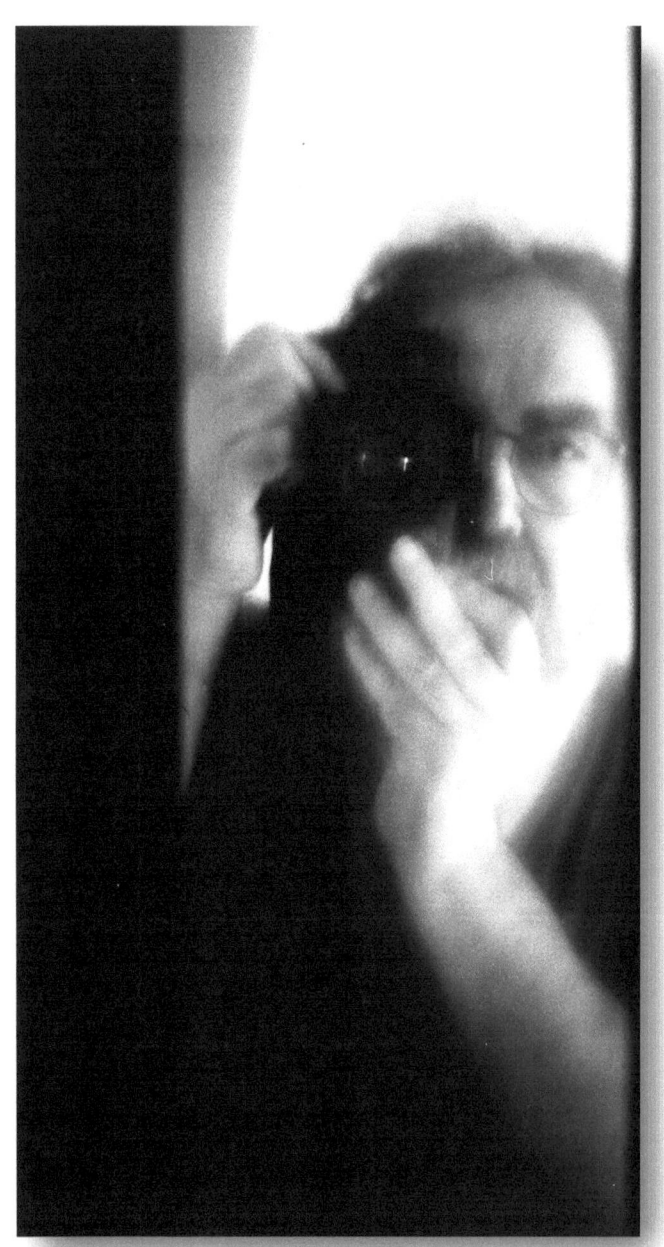

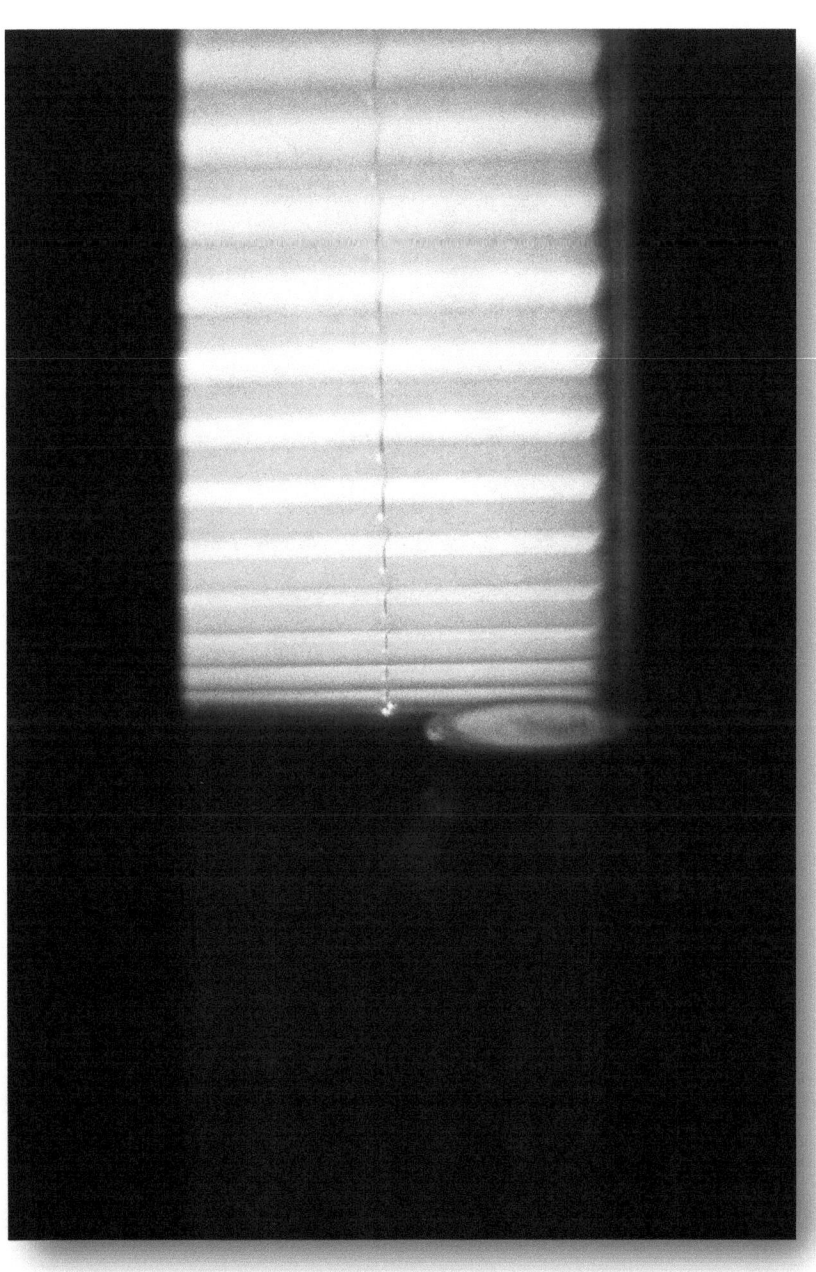

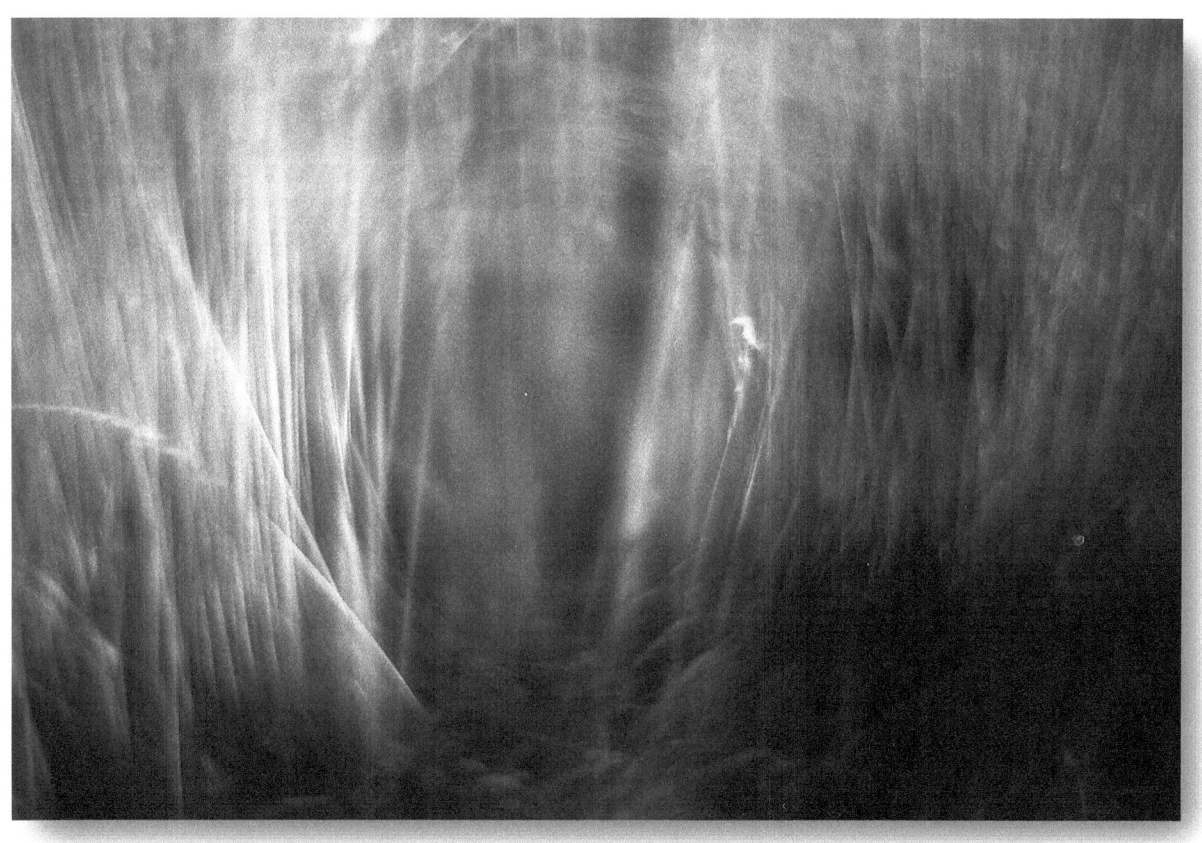

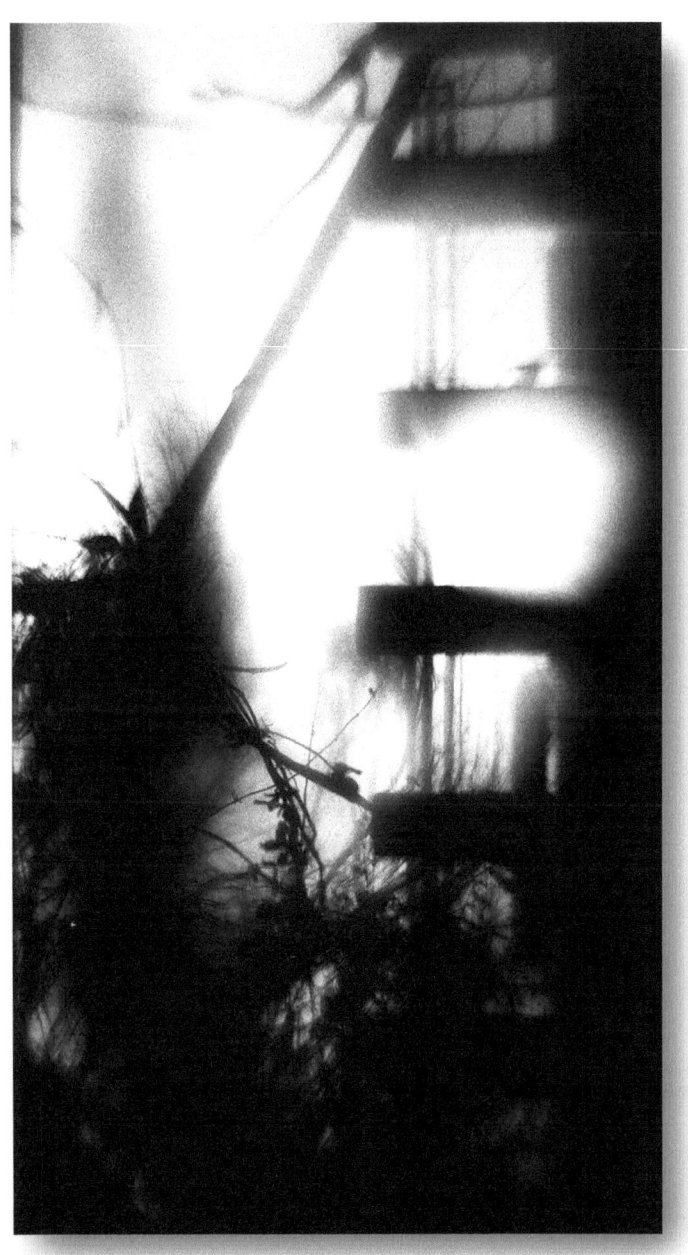

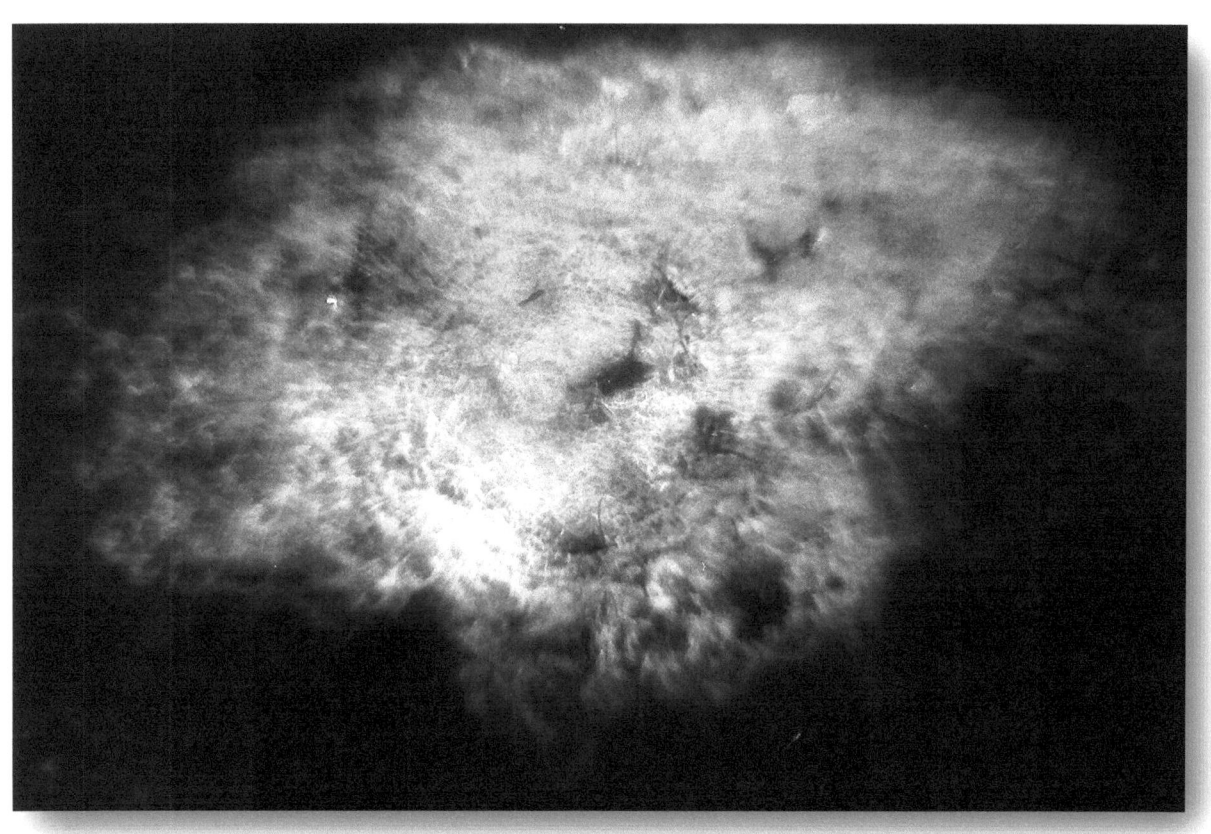

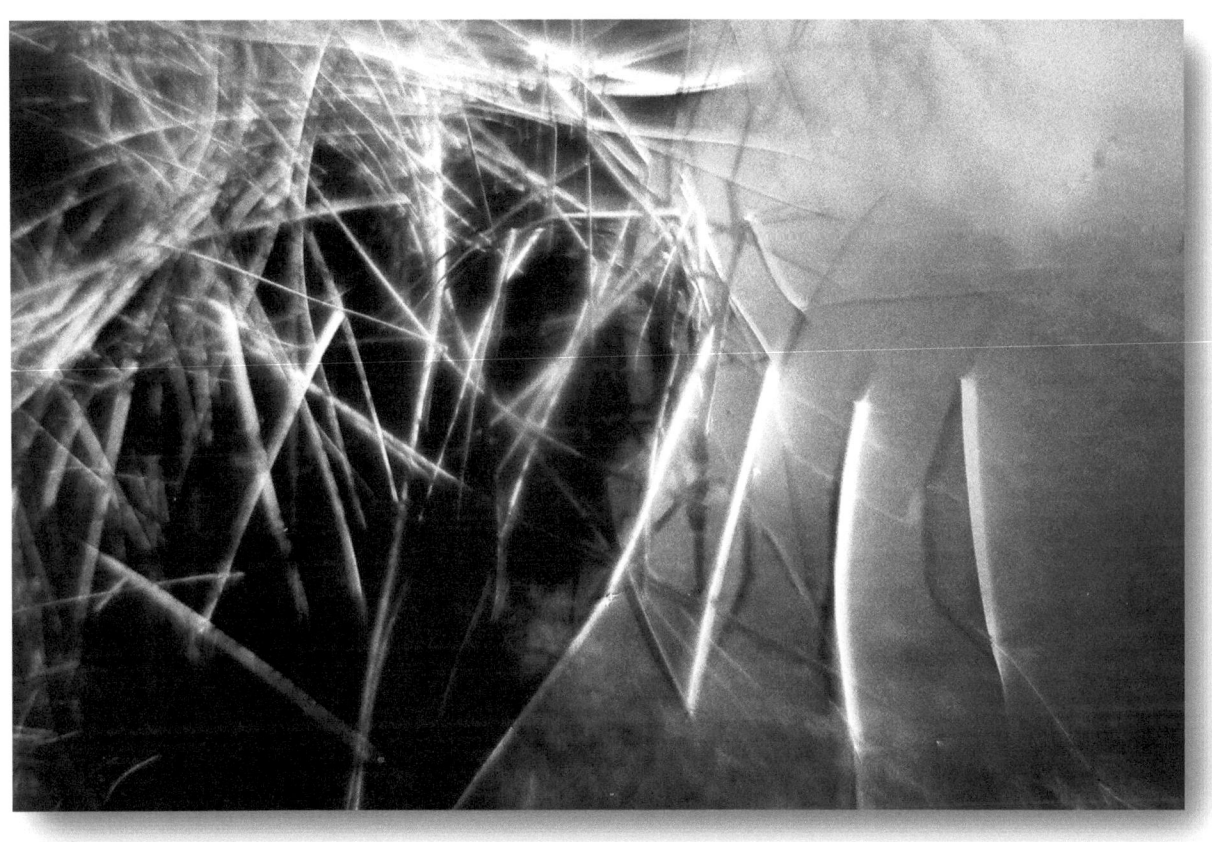

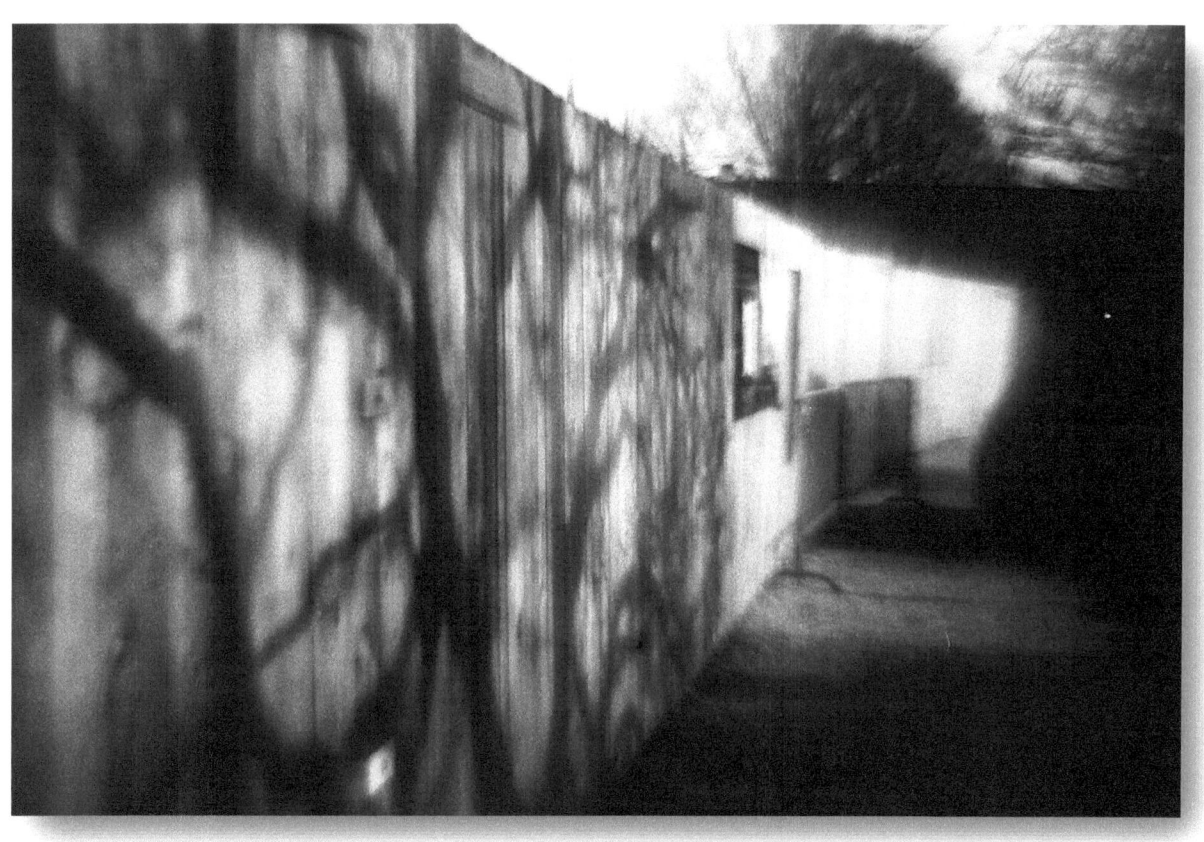

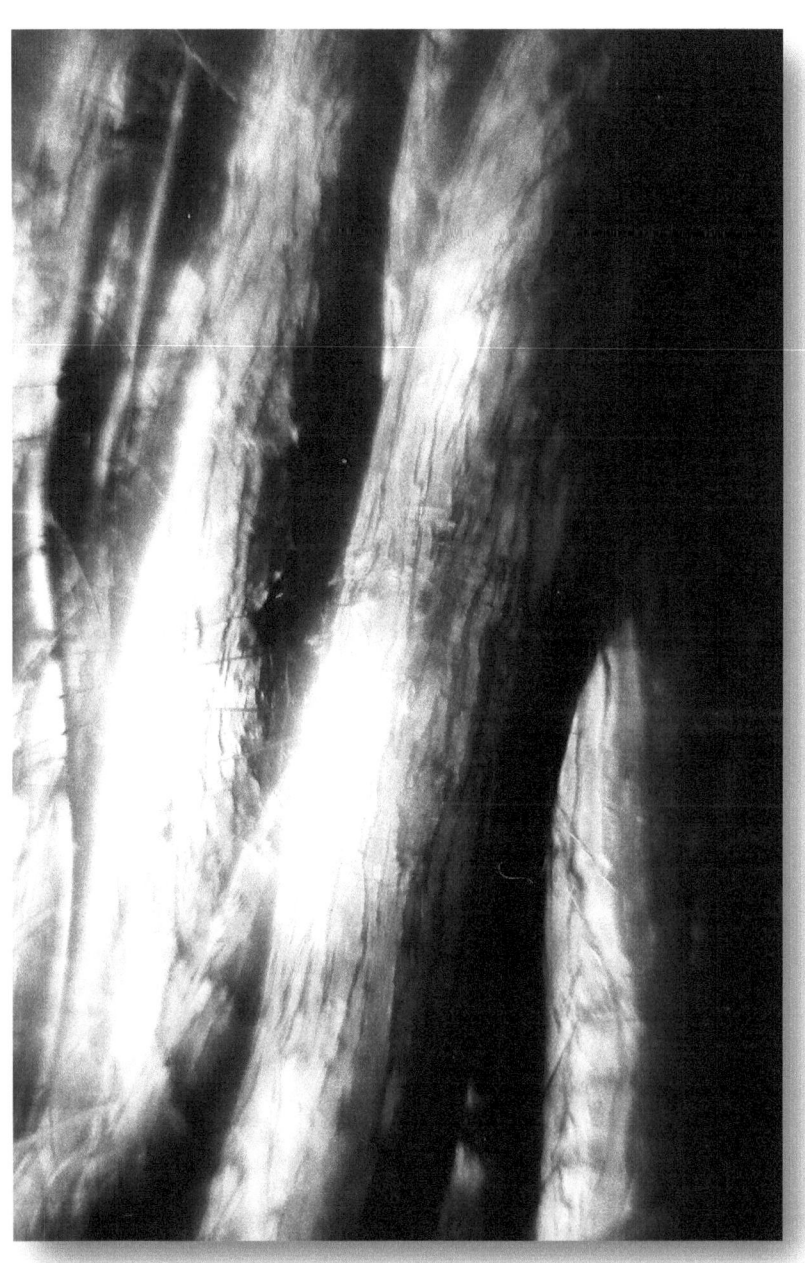

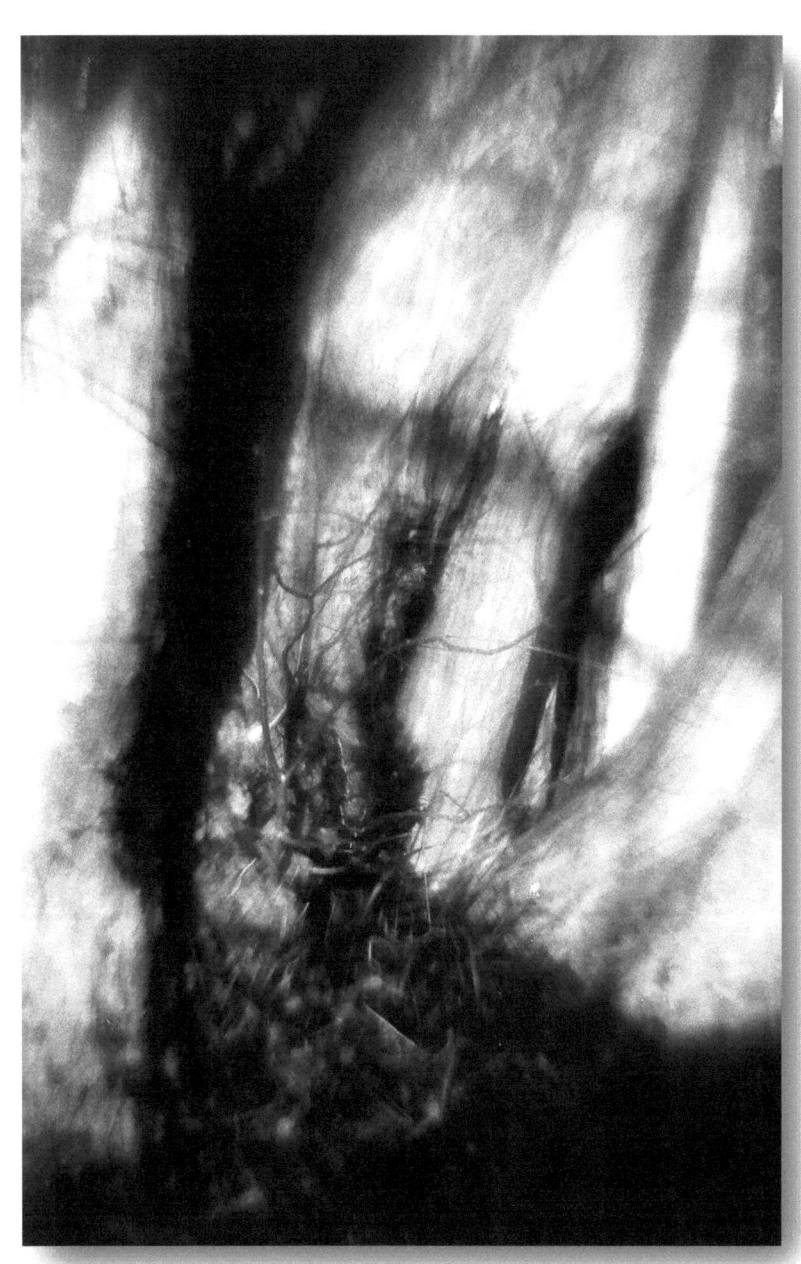

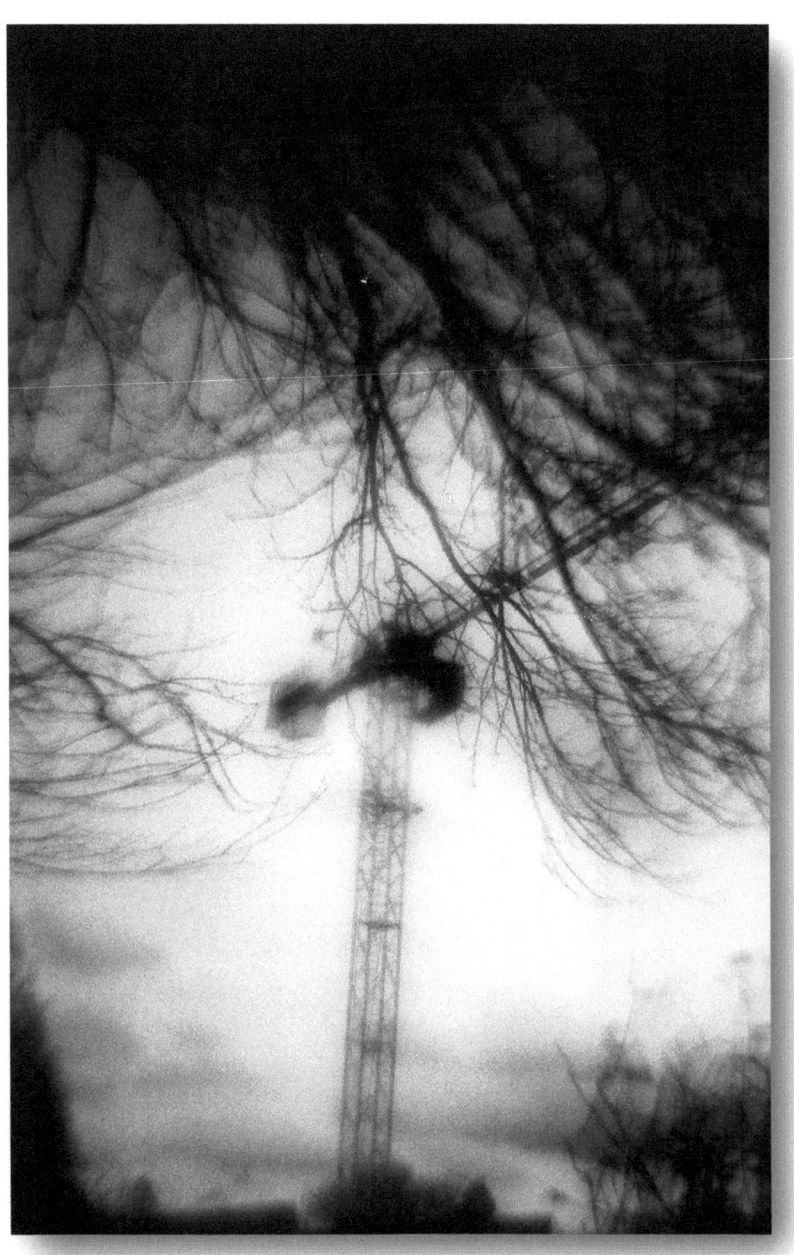

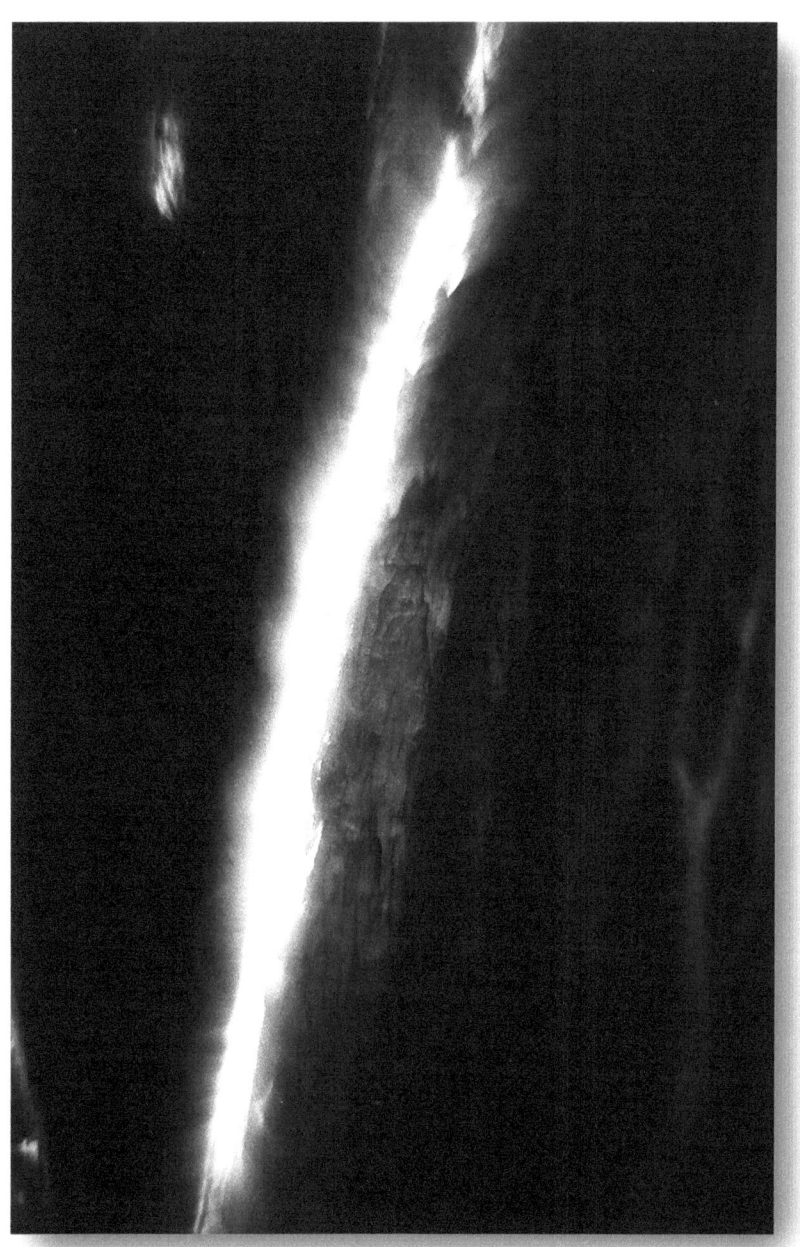

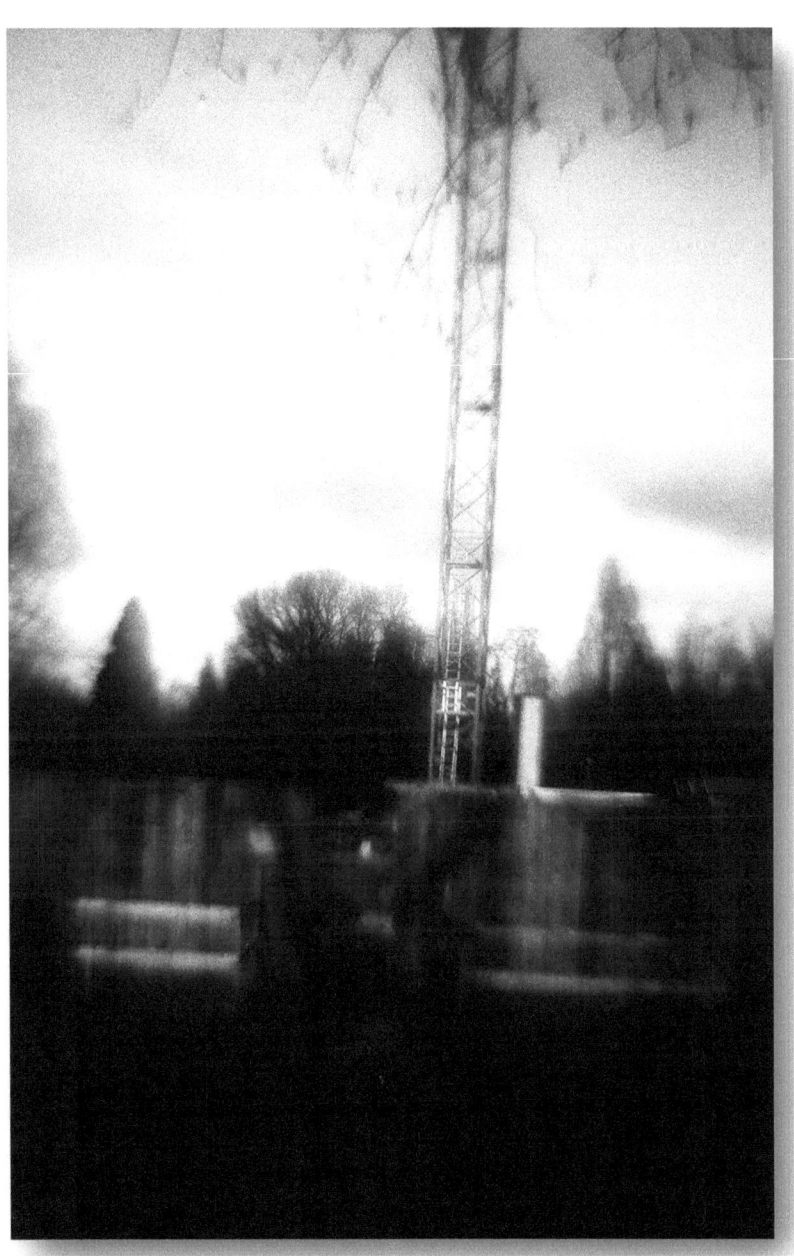

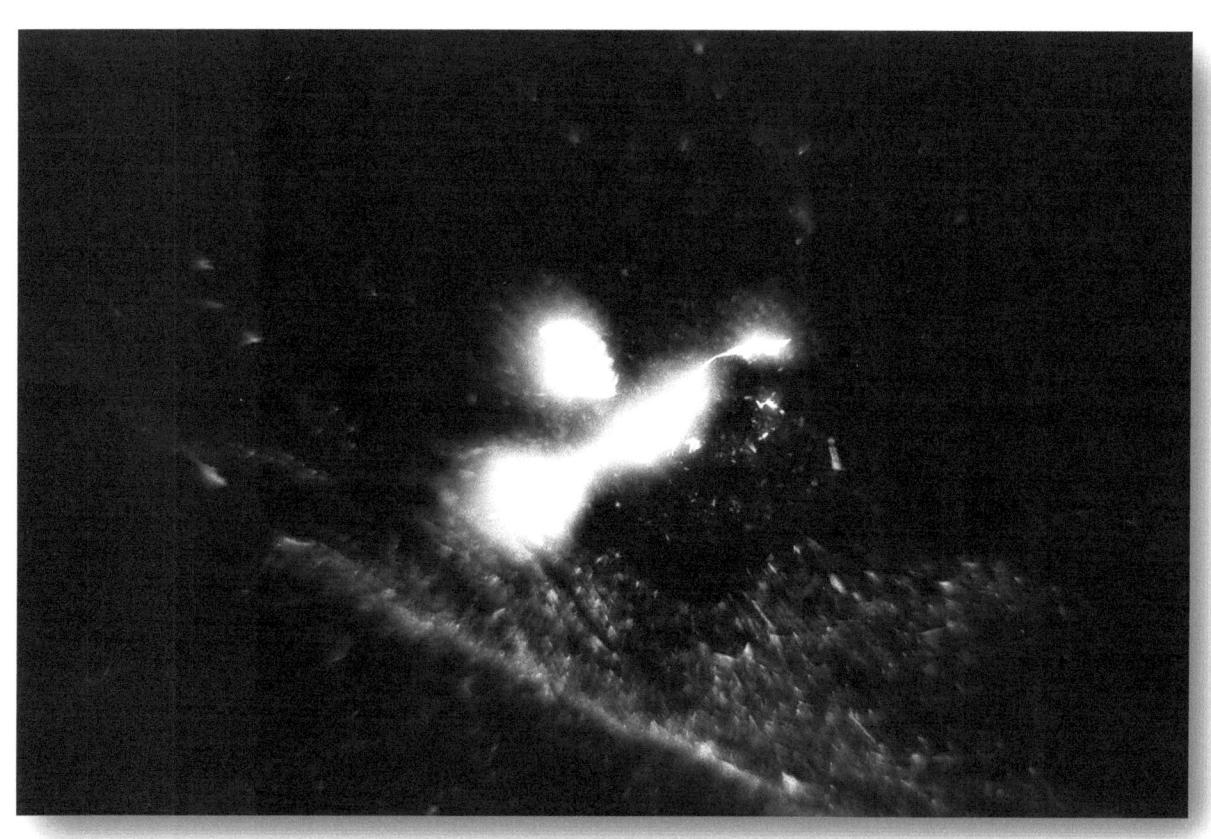

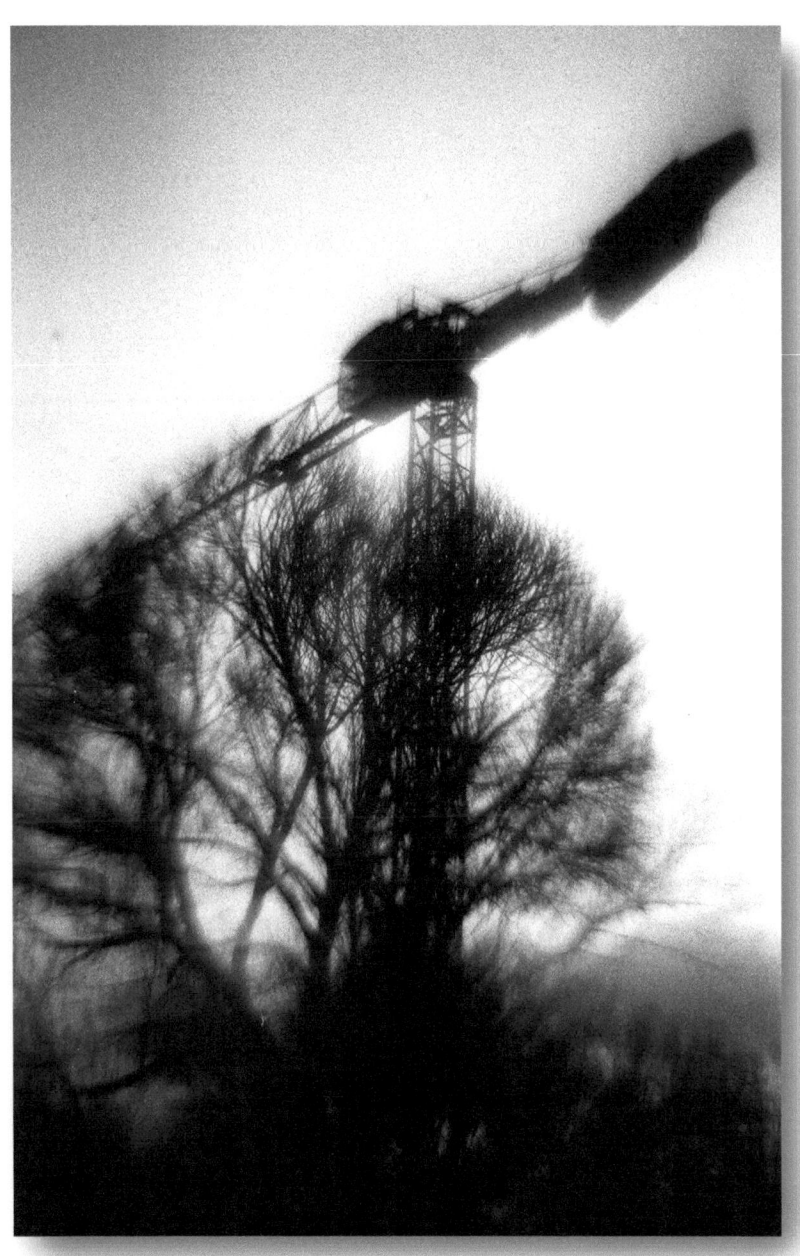

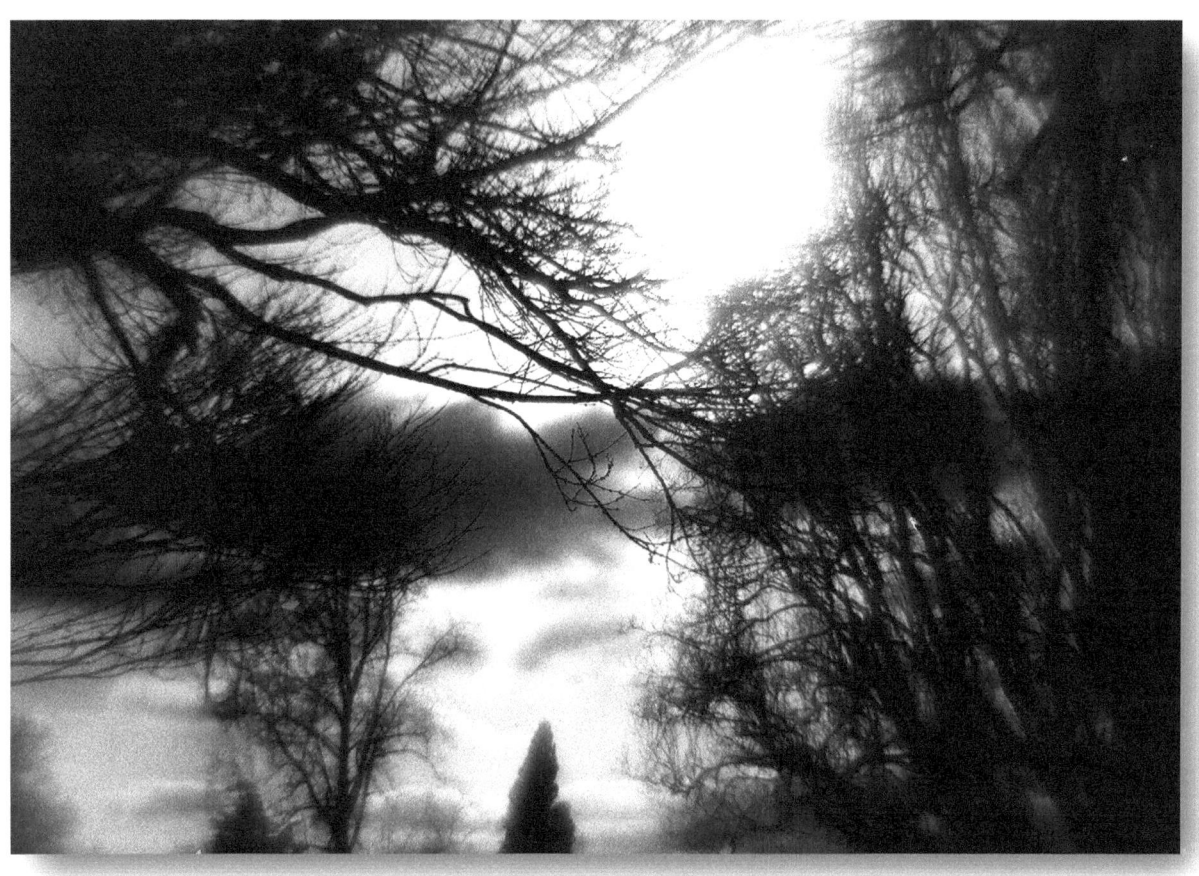

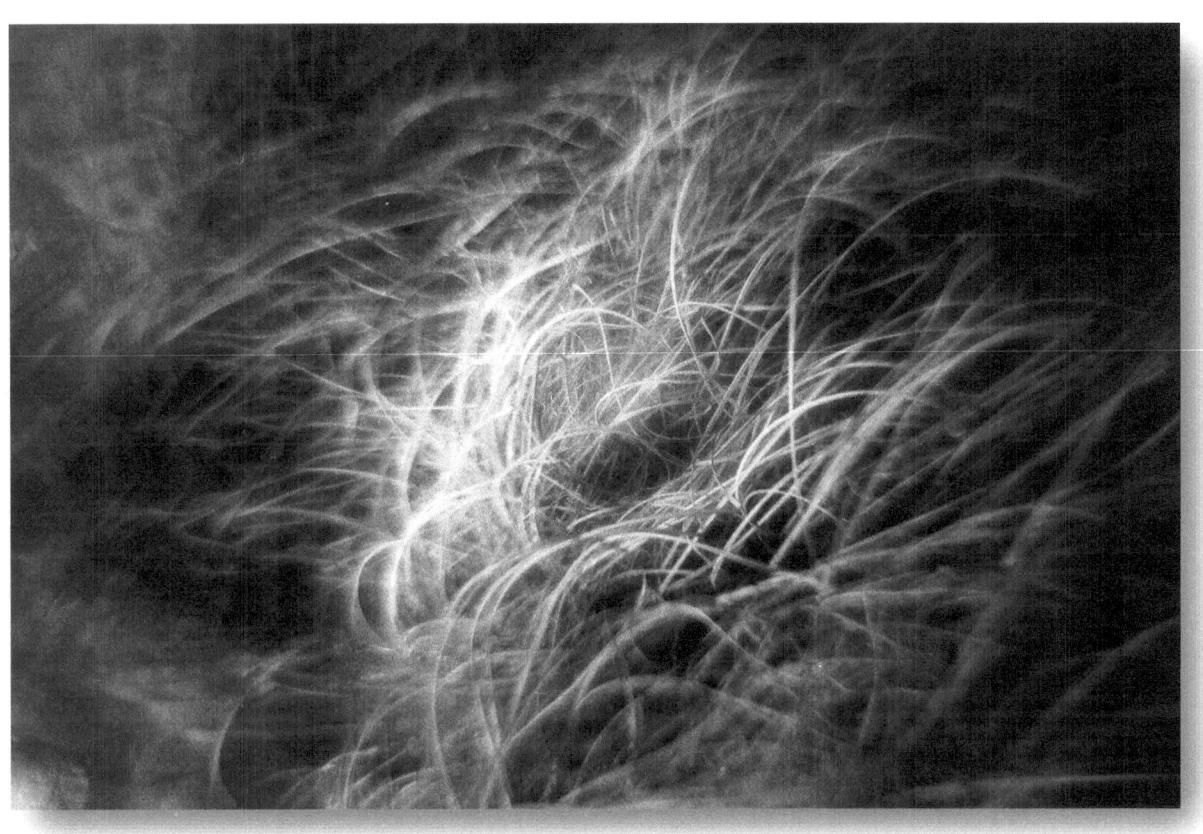

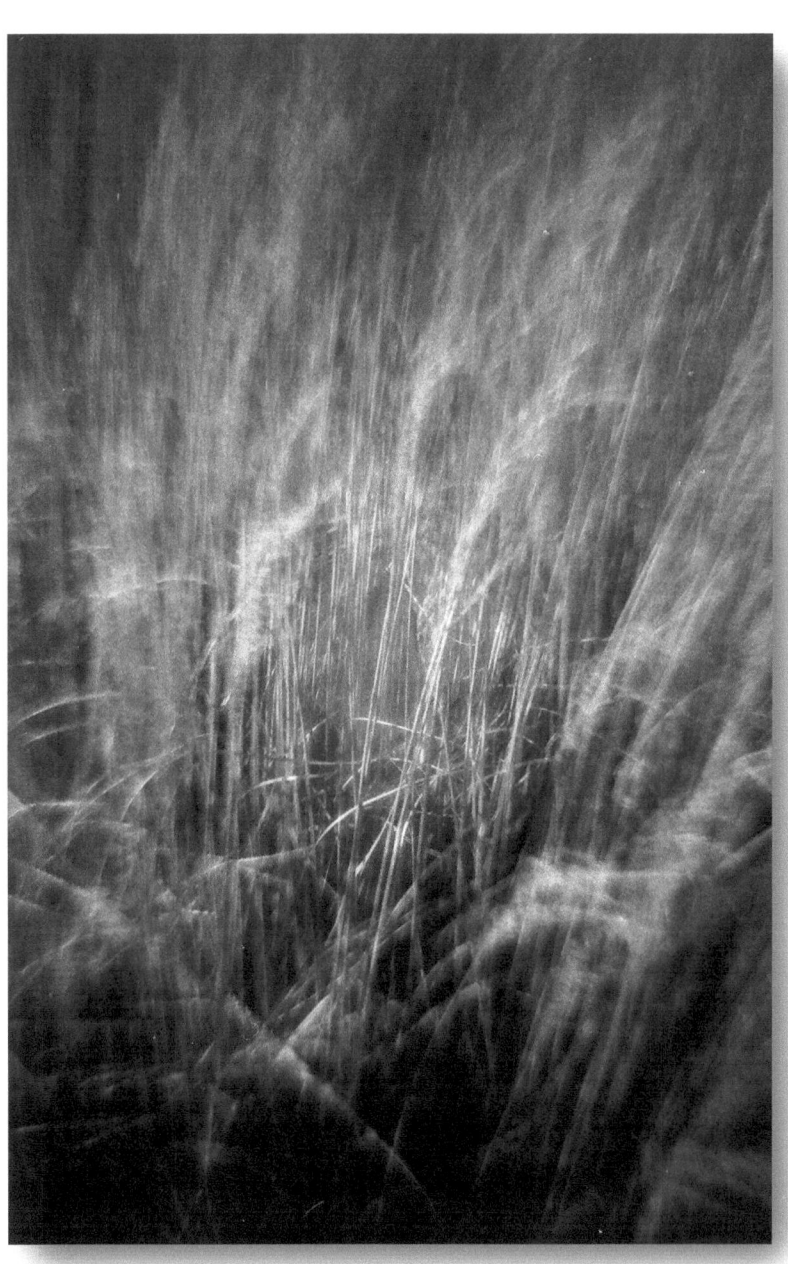

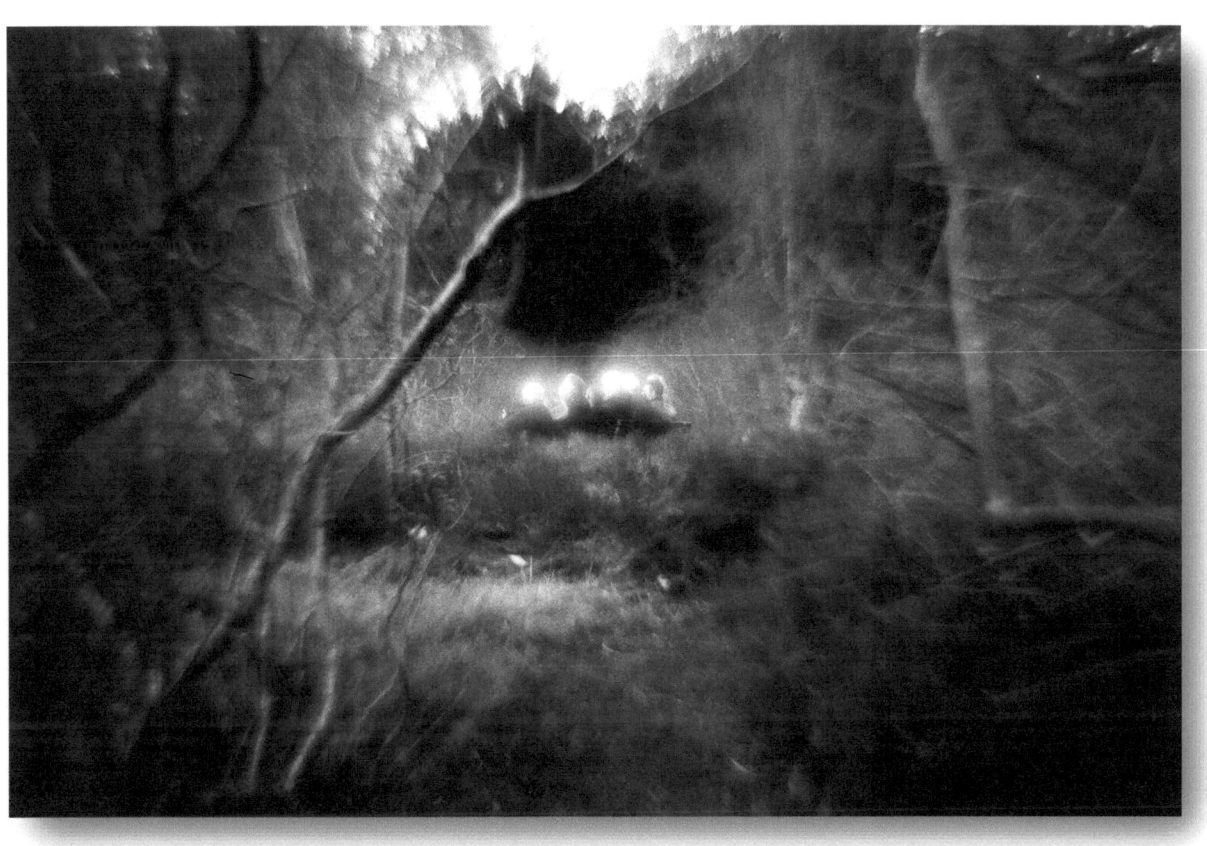

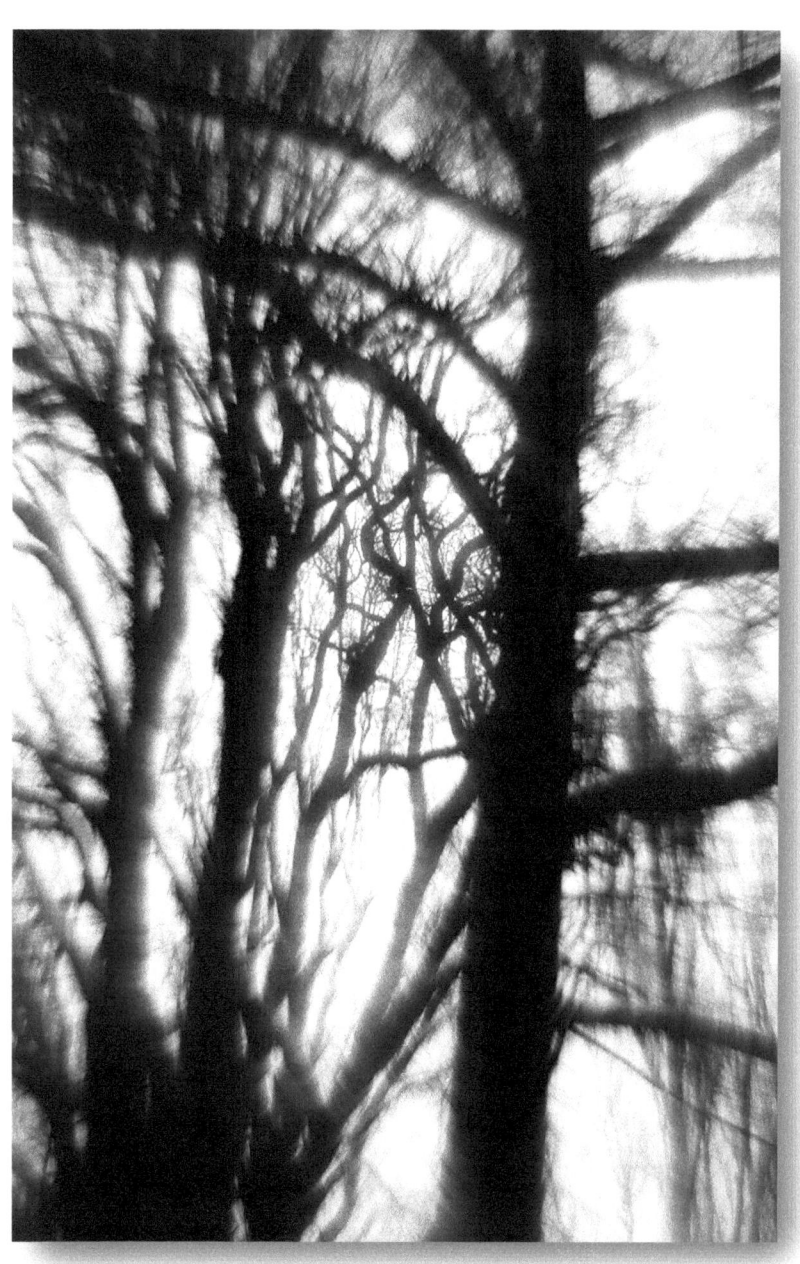

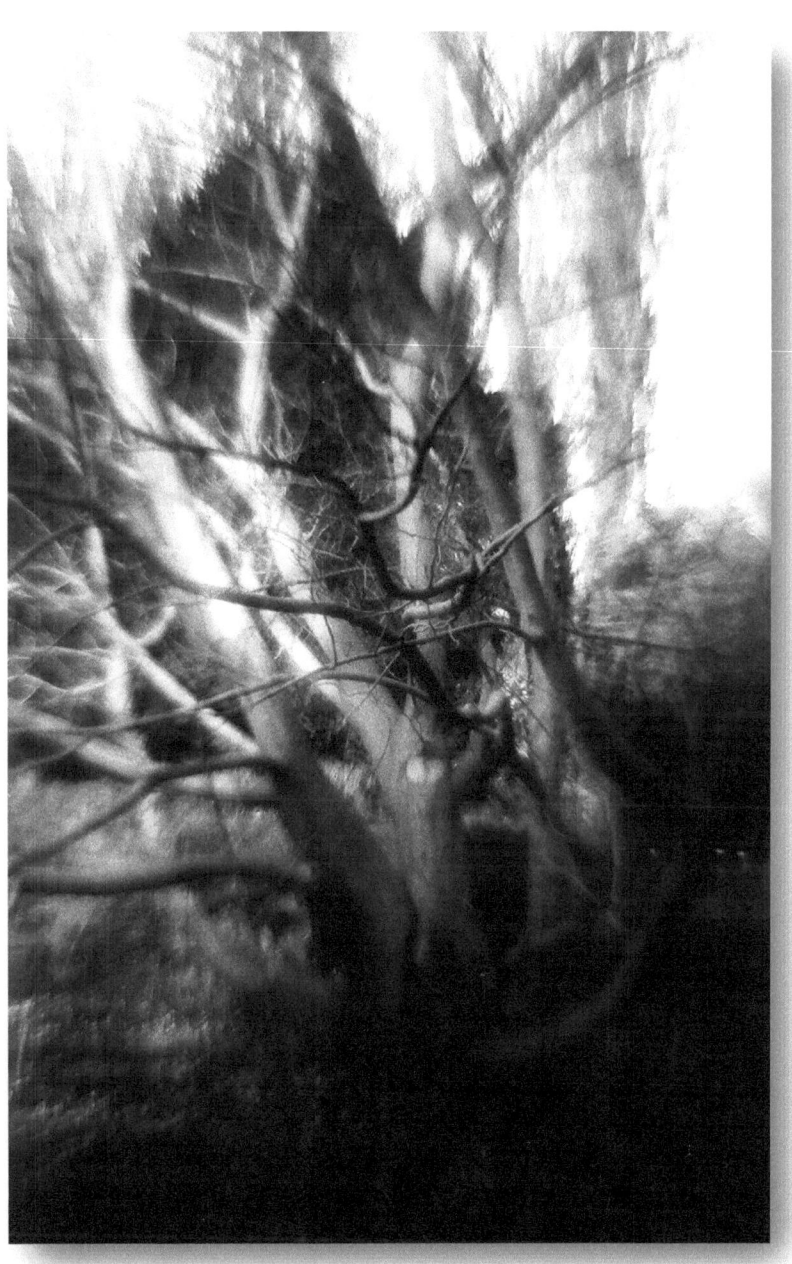

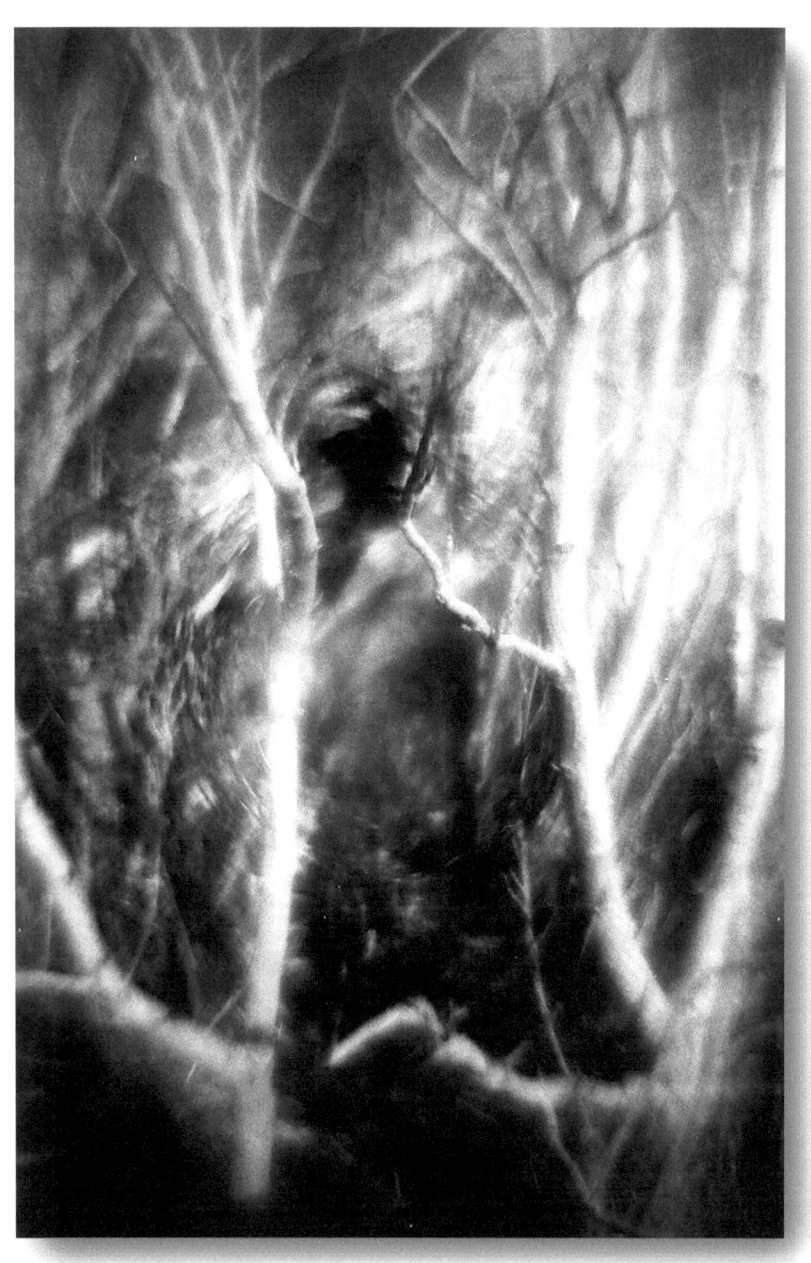

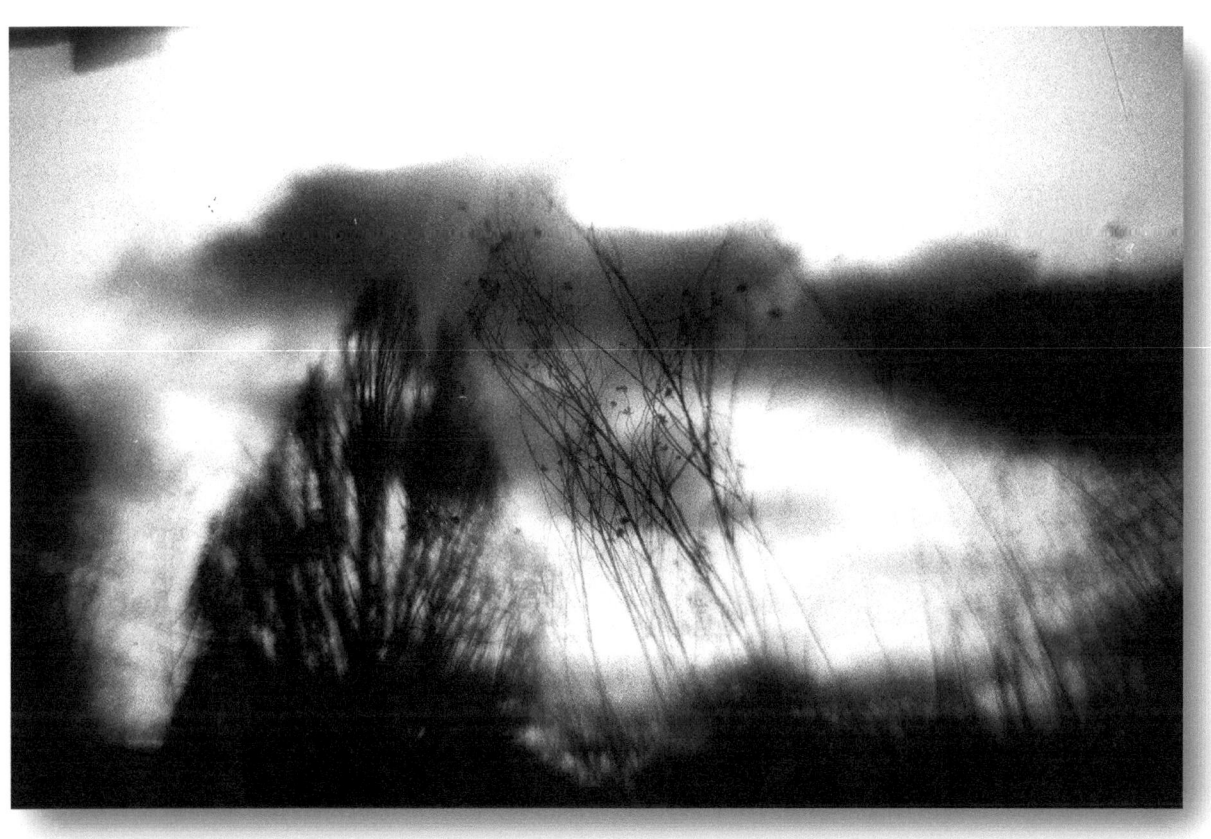

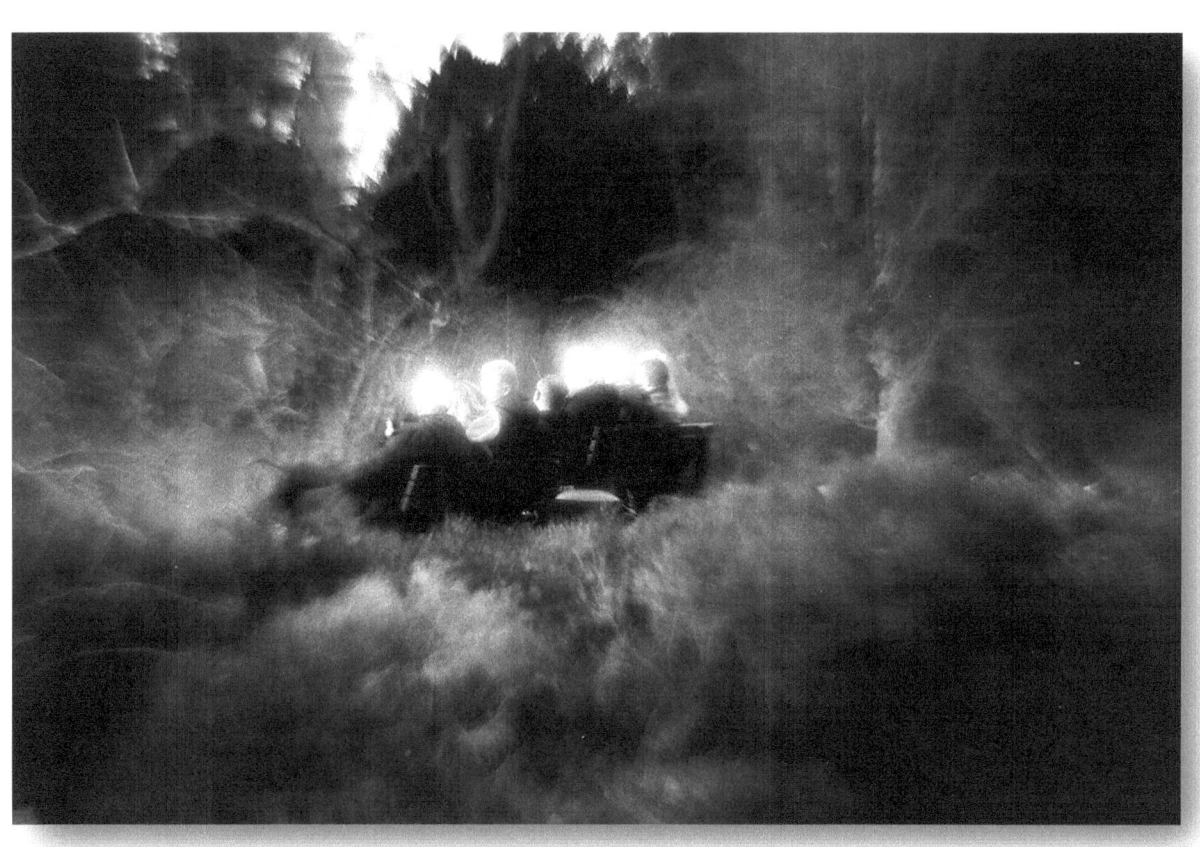

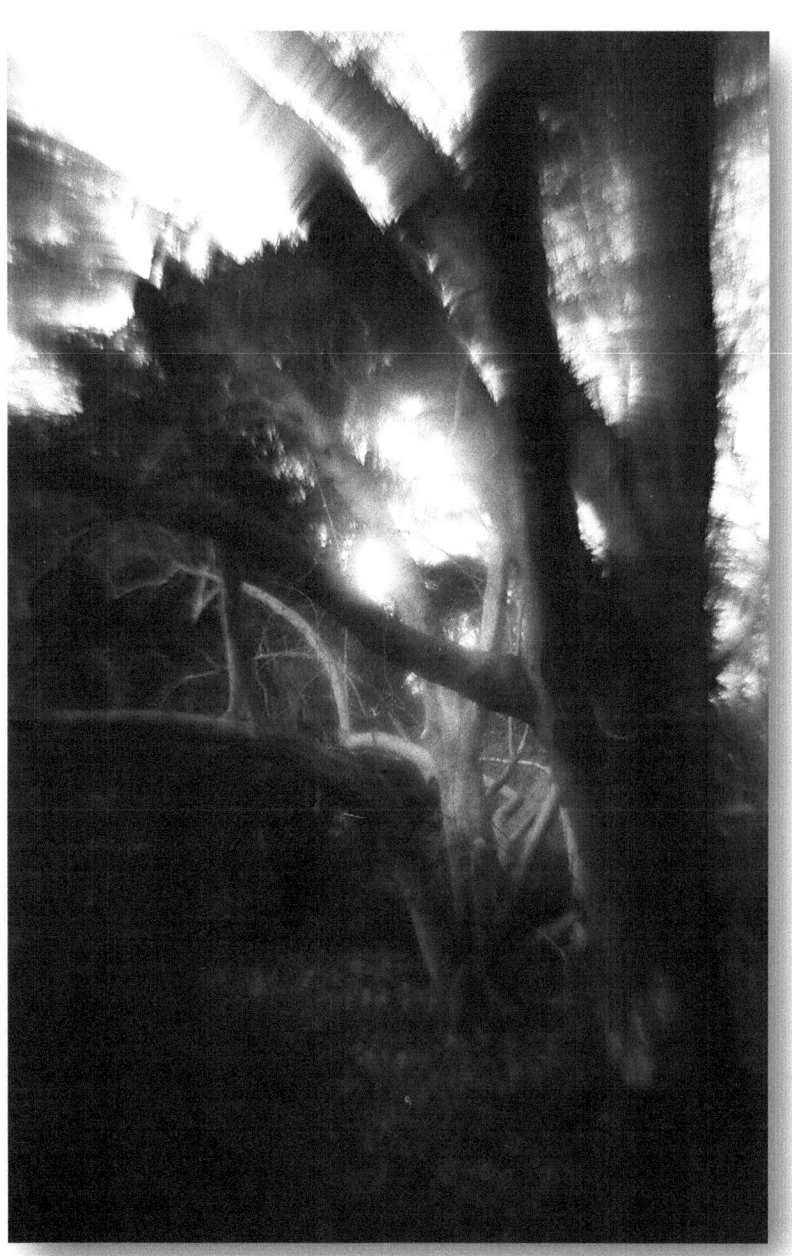

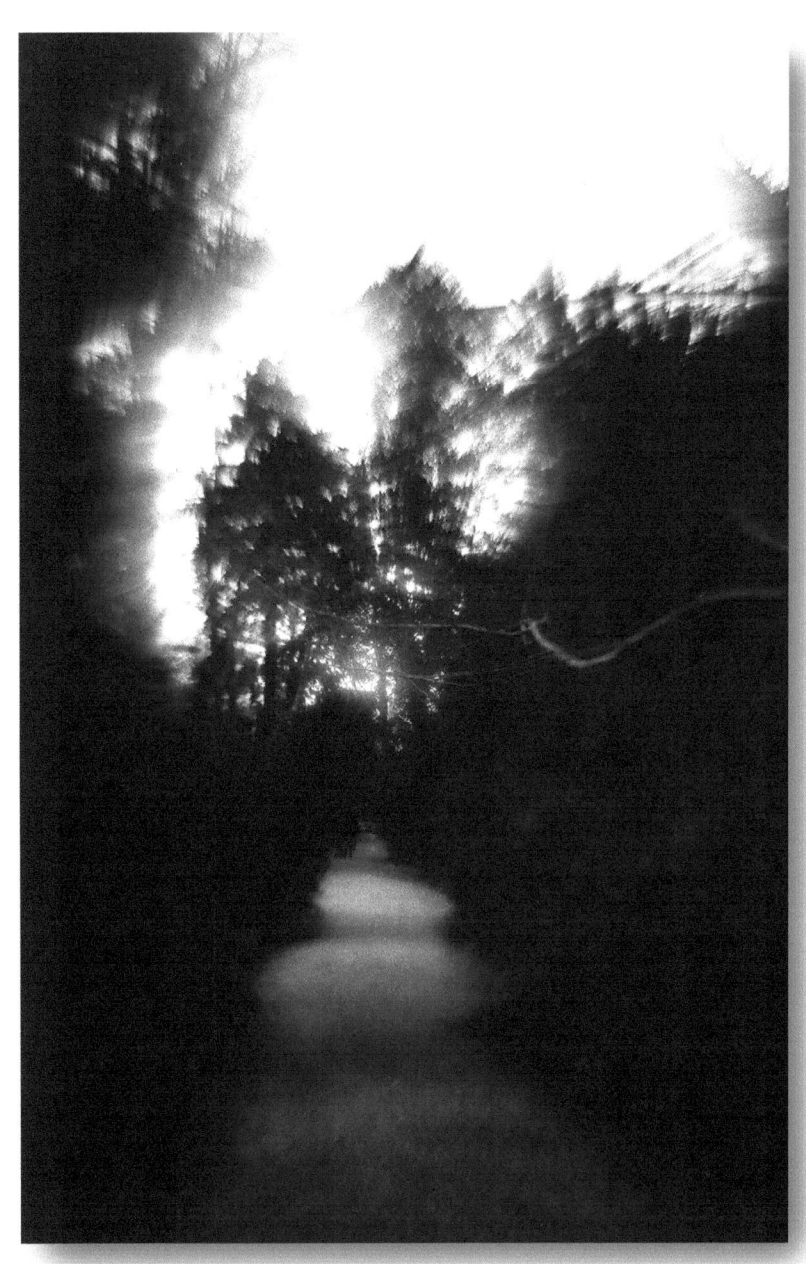

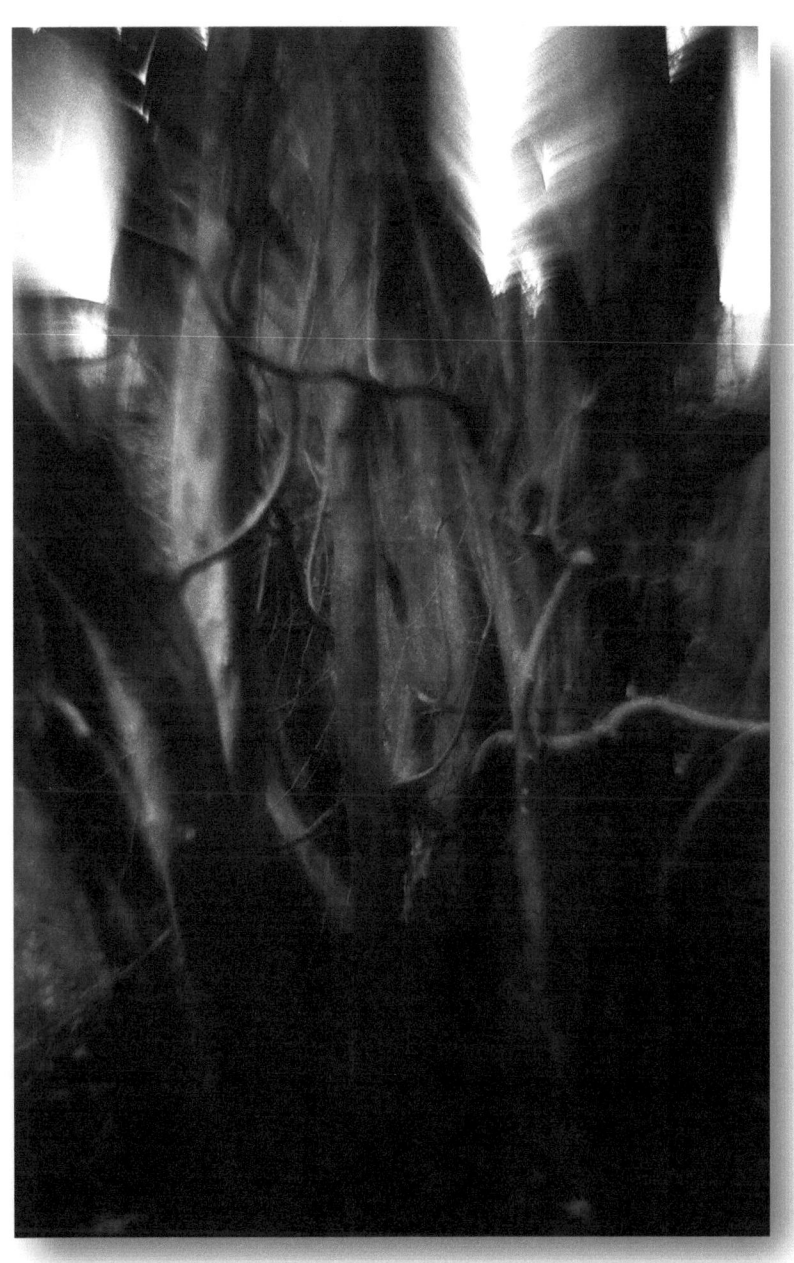

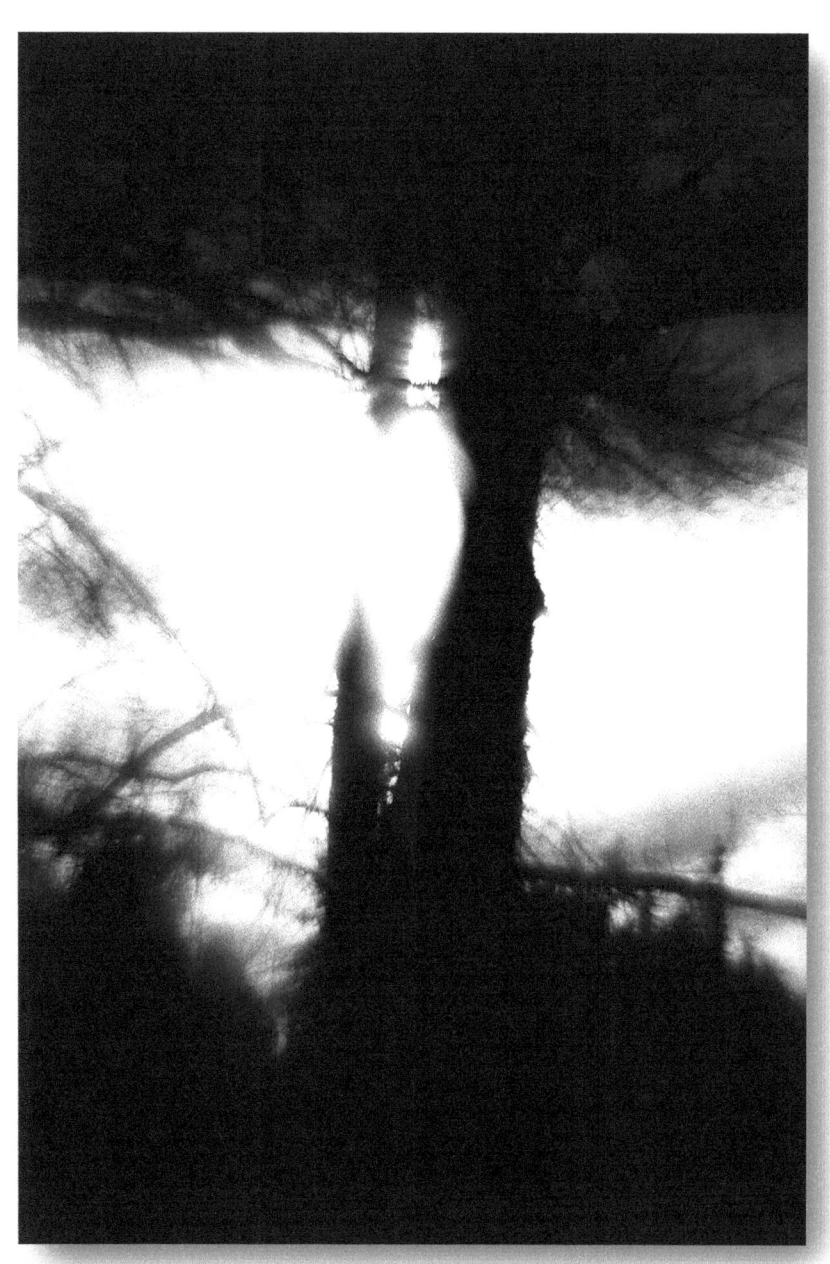

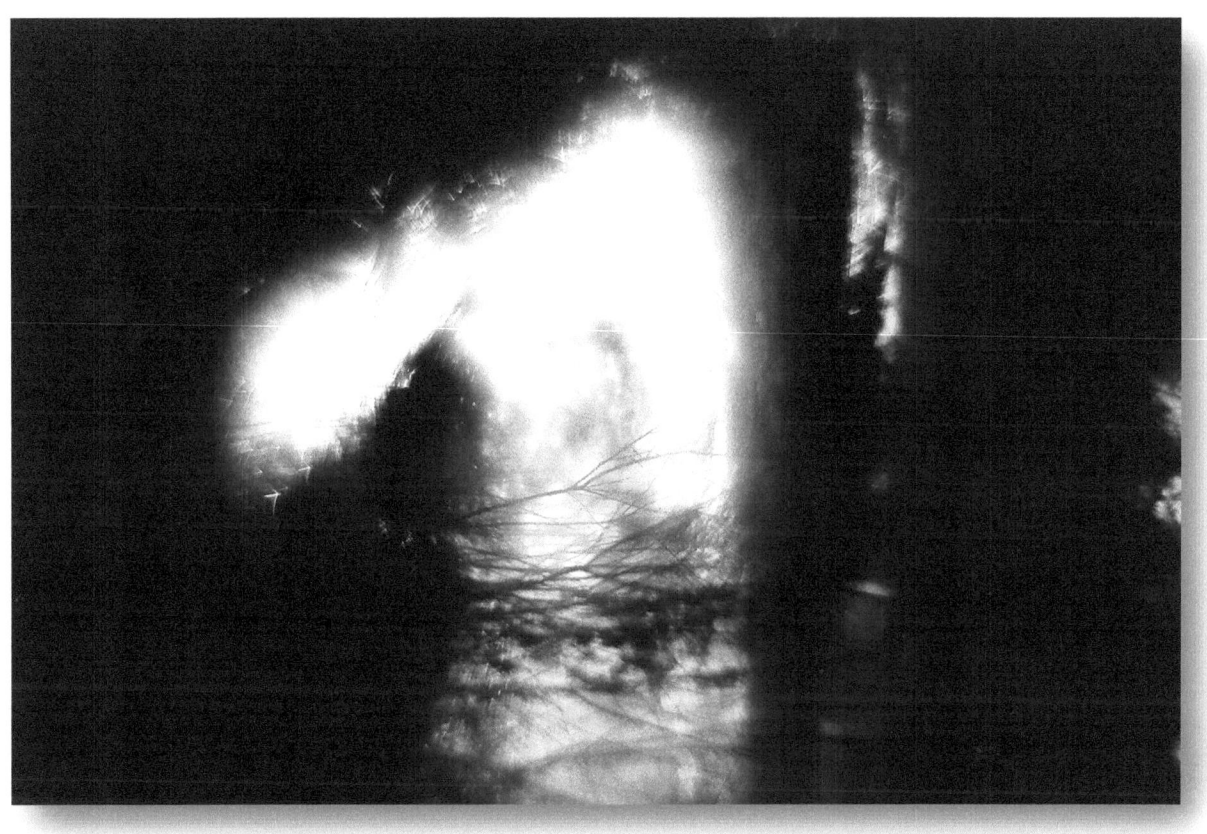

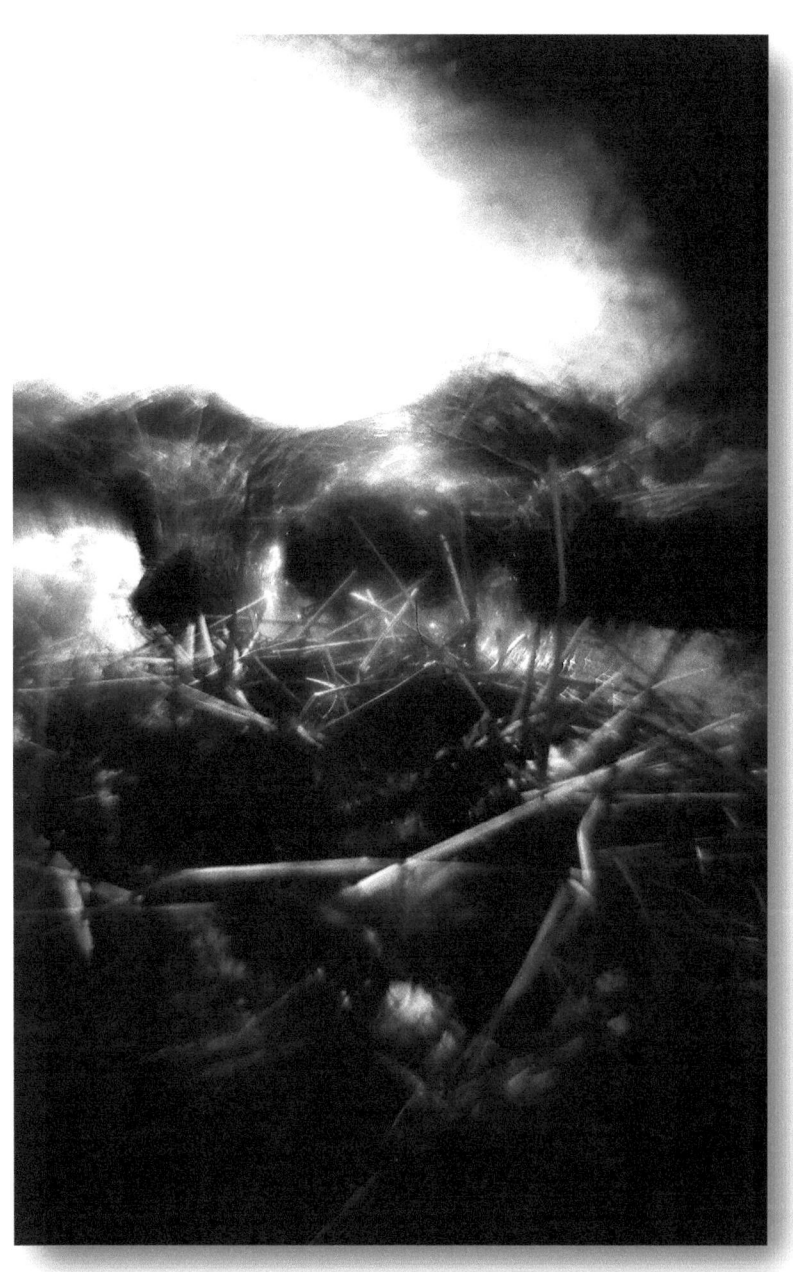

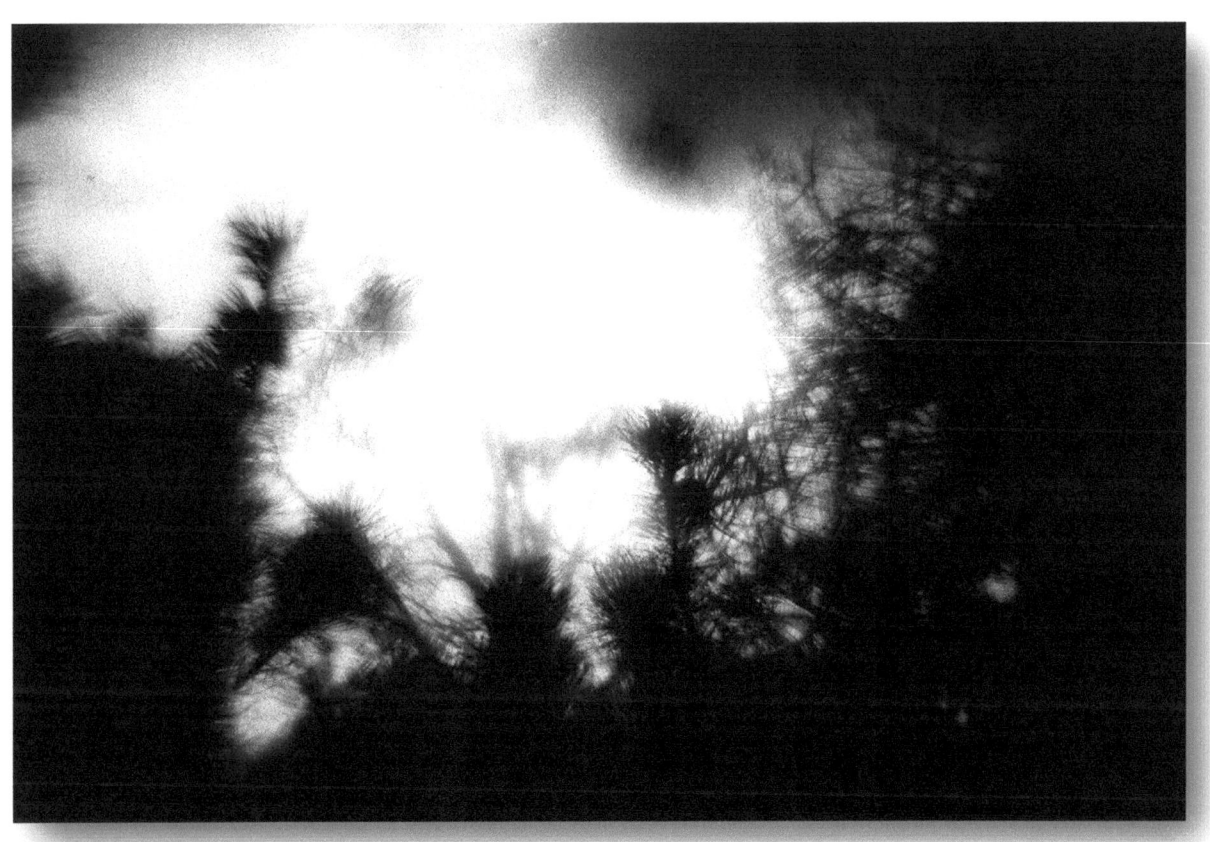

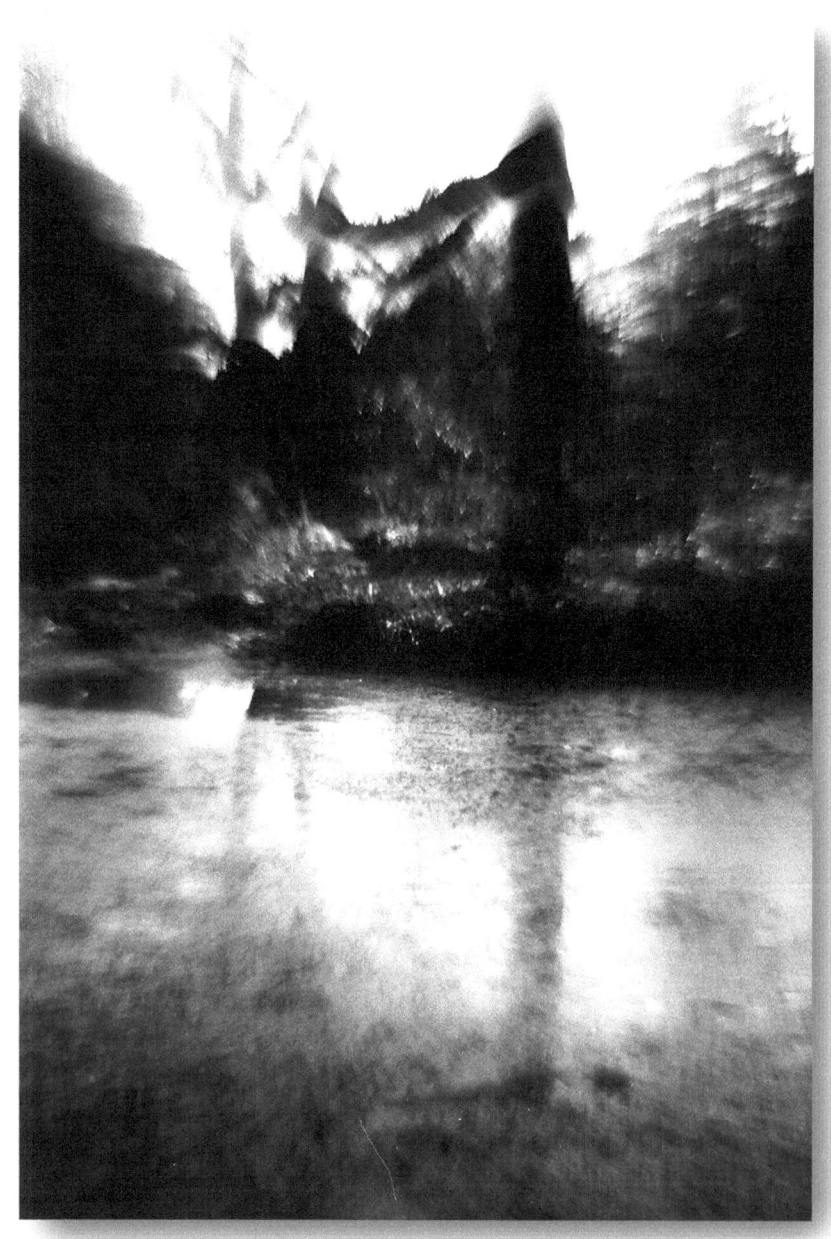

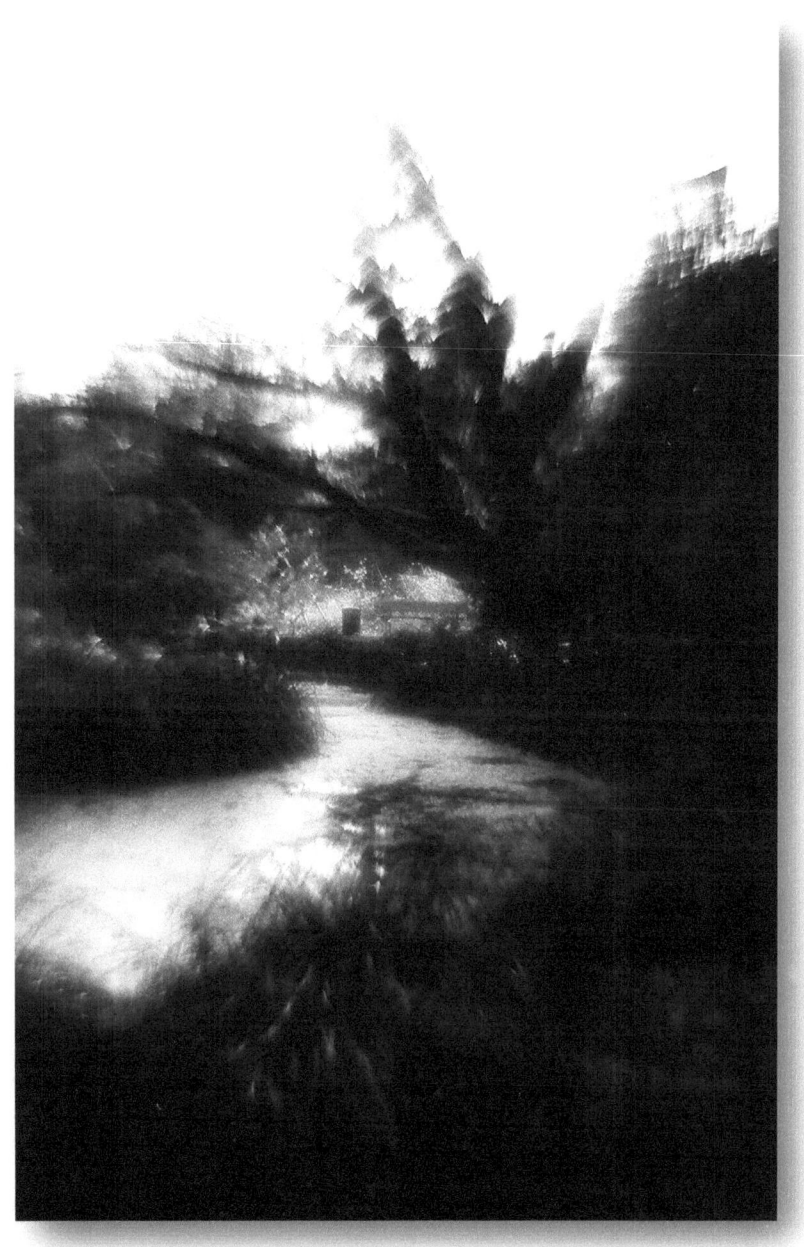

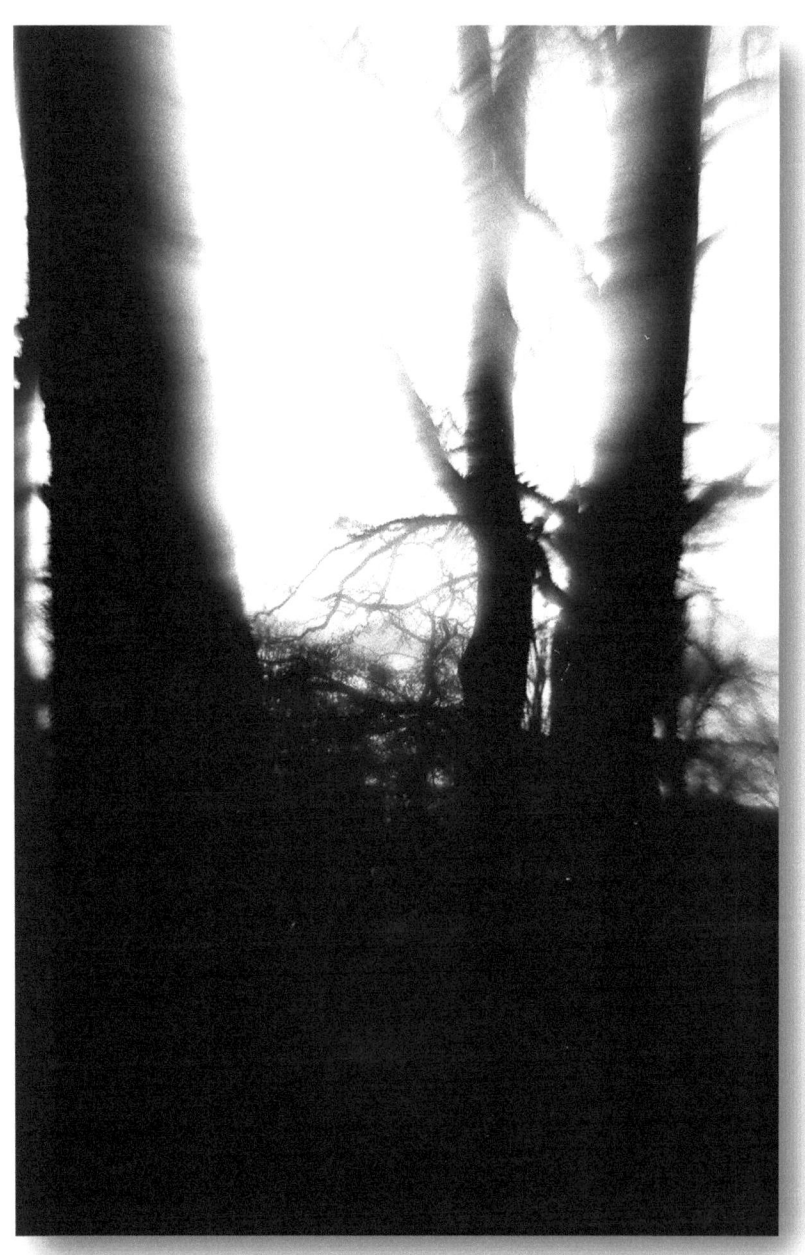